I0517038

A Life Remembered

GLORIA M. MADDEN

ISBN 978-1-957582-38-2 (paperback)
ISBN 978-1-957582-39-9 (eBook)

WESTPOINT
PRINT AND MEDIA

Dedicated
to my
Mother and Father

CONTENTS

1

WISHES COME TRUE

I awoke at seven a.m. on a Monday morning to my radio alarm clock. Turning over on my other side, tucking the blanket around me and grudgingly opening my eyes, there begins to appear a lovely delicate light in hues of yellow and orange streaming thru the curtained window across the bedroom. The sunshine filtered by the large shade tree outside my window and by the nylon curtains blowing softly from the early morning breeze. The bedroom window is left open every night from June thru October to enable me the enjoyment of clear, clean air flowing around the room. The smell of early morning blossoms from the flowerbeds along the walkways lingers in the breeze. Beginning at the front sidewalk, the flowerbeds circle around to the back door, then wind in a semi-circle following the driveway to our two-car garage, they form a maze, a pattern of bright colors edged in green leaves.

As I allow myself a period of luxury, relaxing before starting another busy day at the office, semi-consciousness takes over, I find myself drifting back in time–back to my childhood. Back to the era when my parents purchased our home.

Mother and Father had been looking for a house that would both suit their pocketbook and their ideas on what a sensible – well-built home should have.

1

Father was hoping to find one that had a large cellar that he could turn into a hobby shop and of course a good size garage to keep our station wagon and garden tools in, and, of course a large wrap-around porch for those hot summer nights. Mother was hoping to find a house with enough bedrooms in case Aunt Sophie came for a visit.

Father said it would have to be built well–not that all homes weren't well built–but that my family believed in the basic needs of life and very little luxuries. My family was not poor but they were not well to do neither. I guess we were considered middle class.

Father worked for the railroad as a conductor. I was always so proud to see him in that dark blue uniform with the high round cap on his head. Every morning Mother packed both of us a good lunch, never forgetting to include a piece of cake or candy as a sweet treat. He would have breakfast with us, give Mother and me a hug and kiss, pick up his lunch pail from the table, put on his cap and tell Mother he would be home by six p.m. Then he would turn to me and say, "have a good day at school–mind your manners–and do your chores when you get home".

Mother was the typical homemaker. She loved cleaning and sprucing up the house. She always had fresh curtains on the windows that she cleaned every week with Ammonia and old newspapers. There was always something baking in the oven that sent aromas all thru the house and out the open kitchen window into the yard.

I drifted back to the day my parents had purchased the homestead. The three of us had risen early on a Saturday morning. Mother always made hot biscuits that we devoured with one of her homemade preserves, and a good hot cup of chocolate on Saturdays. After breakfast, I helped with the dishes and made my bed. Father went out to the garage to check the oil and water in the car. Mother and I locked the doors on our way out and waited while Father backed the old station wagon out of the garage and down to the curb.

My family had always rented a big rambling house. One with bedrooms upstairs, with large windows. Now it was going to be our turn to own our home. My parents had spoken on the subject of how to find their house and had decided just to ride around different areas of town going up and down streets that they thought were attractively kept, with trees, gardens and neatly mowed lawns. Hoping they might see a "FOR SALE" sign in the area.

We must have been cruising the area for hours when Mother saw a sign on a front lawn. Father eased the car over to the curb and turned off the engine. It was a lovely neighborhood. All the housed were well taken care of–there were no messy properties–the lawns were all cut and side areas trimmed. The entire street was lined on both sides and lovely large trees, with big leaves, giving lots of shade from the hot sun.

Father suggested that Mother and I wait in the car until he inquired about the house. He walked up the sidewalk, up the front steps and knocked on the door. We watched from the car as Father spoke to the man of the house, then he motioned for us to join him. After we were properly introduced, I pleaded with Mother that I could wait outside while the grownups talked.

First of all, I walked around the large open porch that continued from the front of the house and went around the side of the house. There were steps there too. So I jumped down them one at a time, all six of them. I went back to the front, up the steps and tiptoed along the porch which led to the other side of the house–but no steps. This was really a lot of fun. I decided to explore the yard. Much to my surprise there were flower gardens lining the narrow sidewalk that led around the house, followed the curved driveway, up to the garage. There were so many different flowers, different colors, and different smells. I remember a lovely large shade tree that my eyes followed to the uppermost branches. It was much taller than the two-story house and the branches reached out across the entire back yard.

As I gazed in wonder at that tree, I heard my Mothers voice. She was calling me to come back to the house. We said our goodbyes to the owner and left. All the way home Mother and Father discussed the house. Was it really the right one? Could we afford it? The answer to both questions was a unanimous YES! All weekend the topic of discussion was the house we had seen. It was decided that Monday morning Father would take one of his vacation days from work. At nine p.m. I was reminded it was bedtime. I kissed my parents goodnight, went upstairs, took my bath, put on clean pajamas and climbed into bed.

Monday morning came noon too soon for us. Mother and Father were already dressed and, in the kitchen, when I came downstairs. I excused myself and ran back upstairs to get washed and dressed as quickly as I could. As I came back down the stairs, I almost tripped over our pet cat Patches. I ran into the kitchen and sat down at the table. We had our usual weekday breakfast of juice, cereal and milk. Of course, I wasn't allowed coffee yet to finish off the meal. But that large pot that Mother perked every morning sure smelled good. I helped with the dishes while Father took care of putting some papers together in a business case.

Mother and I locked up the house and waited outside by the driveway for Father to back the car out of the garage. We climbed into the car, settled back, while Father proceeded out the driveway and down the street toward town. He found a parking place in front of the bank and eased our car between two big sedans.

We got out of the car and proceeded to go into the bank. I think we were the first customers of the day. Once inside, Father approached a clerk and asked for the manager. We were escorted to the rear of the bank and into a small office with a large glass door. Seated by a very large desk was a man almost as old as my Father. My Father introduced himself and Mother and I. Then squarely and pointedly right to the purpose we were here, he explained about the loan we needed, the house we wanted and how much a month he could pay on a home loan. Of course, if that amount was all right with the manager. He told the man about his job, salary and how he would continue to work until retirement and toward a pension. He assured the banker that he would keep the house in good condition and even improve it in some areas. Father stated that we were hard working citizens of the community and church going people.

After listening for some time, the bank manager took some forms out of the desk drawer, reached across the desk and handed them to Father. The forms were to be filled out and signed and returned to the manager by Friday. My parents were assured that bank officers would give their request the utmost consideration and in all probability the loan would be handled in a positive manner. My parents thanked the manager and the three of us left his office, walked out the bank and got back into our car.

On the way home we stopped at our local grocery store. Mother shopped for the week's food supplies while Father browsed around the hardware counters. Before we left the store, Mother bought me five cents worth of my favorite chocolate candy. The grocer had a helper. He was one of my classmates. I think he was hired to sweep the floor, stock the shelves and make deliveries. His name was Butch, I never could remember his last name. Butch helped carry the grocery bags out to our station wagon and placed them on the floor in the rear area by the tailgate. When we arrived back at our house Father took the grocery bags out of the car and placed them on the back steps by the kitchen door. He put the car in the garage while Mother and I carried the bags into the house and put them on the kitchen counters. I always helped put the can goods and cereals away. Mother took care of the meats and other perishable items. After helping, I excused myself and went upstairs to my bedroom. I changed into my play clothes and then began getting my schoolbooks ready for the next day.

The days went very slowly that week. They seemed to just creep by. I think I was as anxious as my parents about the bank loan. Each night after finishing my homework, taking my bath and getting into bed, I would lie awake listening to them discussing the house we had looked at, figuring out loud the expenses and agreeing with one-another that a mortgage could be handled without straining the budget.

Friday came none too soon. Our school was closed because of a teacher's seminar, so I was allowed to go with my parents to the bank again. I fed our pet cat Patches, brushed his fur and found a piece of yarn from Mother's crochet basket. Patches loved to play "catch it" as I dangled the yarn back and forth in front of him. Mother called me to the table which I had set for her earlier. She had hot chocolate ready for me and hot coffee ready for Father and her. We finished breakfast, cleaned up the kitchen, got dressed up for the trip to town, locked the doors and proceeded to get into the station wagon. Well- there was Patches back into the house. I assured Mother that I had changes the kitty litter in his box. We kept it just inside the kitchen door in a corner that had been a small storage are with two small doors and a window seat on top.

We continued our trip to town. It was a beautiful spring morning. The trees had new green leaves, the sun was shining and playing with the streaks of light that cascaded thru the early morning dew on the leaves. Mother said she was sure that this was to be our lucky day. The streets were already crowded with cars. People were out early to do their holiday shopping. Father was a careful driver and was taking his time weaving thru the traffic. He found the same parking place by the bank, now Mother really felt this was another lucky omen. We got out of the car, locked it up, and proceeded toward the bank door.

Once inside the bank Father asked the clerk to escort us to Mr. J. Jones, the bank manager. Mr. Jones greeted us with a smile and shook hands. Mr. Jones asked us to please sit down and relax. He began to talk about the weather, the upcoming holiday and the banking business. Just a little conversation to help us relax, he said, nothing to start worrying about. The manager took a folder out of his desk drawer and placed it on top of the desk. He opened it and spread out the papers before him. He then spoke about the house we wanted and asked my parents some more questions. The manager then explained the board of directors had met, and with a twinkle in his eyes he congratulated my parents on obtaining the loan and wished us much happiness in our new home. Oh My! We were so thrilled. Just think! Our own homestead! After signing a few more forms Mr. Jones walked us to the front door and again wished us well. As we drove away, we waived goodbye and Mr. Jones waived back.

My parents and I were so excited, we could hardly think about the upcoming holiday. Father said he would treat us to lunch at the little restaurant by the edge of town. We had left the bank just as the guard was ready to lock the doors. Due to the upcoming holiday the local bank was closing at noon. The traffic was really getting heavy now, the people on the sidewalks were walking faster then our car was moving. As we sat waiting for the traffic policeman to beckon us on, Mr. Jones, the bank manager, walked by carrying his briefcase. Our car was finally moving and I settled back in the seat wondering what we would have for lunch.

All the parking places in front of the restaurant were taken so Father drove around the side street and found a space open. As we walked up to the restaurant a waiter ushered us to a table, on the outdoor patio. There were round tables painted white, with large umbrellas fastened to the center of each table. The chairs were white with red and white-checkered seat covers that matched the tablecloth. The entire patio was surrounded by a small white picket fence, and, on the patio along the fence there were big flowerpots full of blossoming geraniums. The waiter had seated me between my parents. While we were waiting for our waiter to return to our table, I glanced up and noticed the edge of the umbrella gently flapping in the breeze making the red and white check pattern dance to and fro. My parents ordered one of the specials for the day. I ordered a hotdog and root beer. After a very enjoyable lunch we proceeded to leave when I noticed Butch, my classmate. He came over, shook hands with

Father and explained he was here making a delivery and hoping that some day he might have a chance to be a waiter. We said goodbye to Butch and wished him and his family a happy holiday.

Mother reminded Father that she needed some special groceries so we stopped at the food store on our way home.

That evening I helped prepare the holiday foods. Mother and I baked a cake, some cookies and two pies. One apple and the other a custard cream. After helping to clean up the kitchen I went into the living room to play with our pet cat Patches. Friday evenings I was always allowed to stay up later than during the week. Father had settled back in his easy chair with his pipe and one of his favorite books. Mother finally sat down and relaxed, picking up her basket of wool, she continued to crochet an alfghan of mixed colors.

I looked up at my parents and thought how lucky we are to have our WISHES COME TRUE.

2

OUR HOMESTEAD

My family moved into the new home one month later. The previous owner had agreed with my Father that one month was sufficient time for him to pack and move out. The man was a widower and wanted to move to be near his son and family.

After the holiday passed, we began packing, sorting out what we no longer wanted from the storage closets, trying not to get in one another's way. My goodness! There were boxes packed, tied and stacked everywhere. This was a perfect time for me to clear out the large walk-in closet where I kept all my games, toys and dolls that had been saved from the time I was in a crib. There was my old brown Teddy Bear in a corner, a scattered puzzle game, some old crayons, a Raggety Ann doll my Aunt Sophie had given me when I was five years old. As I worked my way around the other side of the closet, I found some old Christmas wrapping paper, and, under it there lay the bracelet my teacher had given me when I had my tonsils removed. I searched for that bracelet I misplaced for a long time and was certainly glad I had at last found it. My eyes shifted to a doll crib that held my favorite baby doll and the doll blanket Mother had crocheted. The blanket began to move and I sat frozen with fear thinking it was a mouse or something worse. But from under the cover came our

9

pet cat Patches. He just wanted to play. Oh My! Did I breathe a sigh of relief!

The month went by so fast. The only time I had to help pack was weekends. During the week I had homework every night and Mother and Father made sure I was in bed by nine p.m. After I was tucked in and the bedroom light turned off, I would lie awake listening to the rustle of boxes, cabinet doors opening, sometimes, something falling on the floor, as if Mother had tried to carry too much at one time. Mother had packed everything except one set of dishes, the everyday silverware and what other kitchen pots and pans and utensils she would use for the next few weeks. I had helped Mother on the weekends to sort out the linens, blankets, and pack and label the boxes.

That month I had not seen too much of Father. He was busy sorting out what he had called "junk" in the cellar. He had many tools, large and small that were kept in very large toolboxes. When the car needed a repair or something in the house needed to be fixed, Father was always had the right tools for the job. He even had a tool that sharpened our lawn mower blades. By the end of the month he had a huge pile of junk that had to be hauled away by the town junk-man as they were called then. The junk-man had also taken something that Mother had thrown out. She had packed a large box of clothes that were too small for me, some of her old dresses and coats and some old pants that were too small for Father. She gave this box of clothes to the junk-man to sell. He was very pleased and thanked Mother.

Father had contacted the local moving company during the month. They had sent a man over to see how, much furniture and boxes there were to be moved and then stated what the cost would be. The man had come to our house on a Saturday morning and I couldn't help listening to him as he spoke. He explained to my parents how his workers would cover the furniture before it was loaded on the truck. This assurance made Mother feel much more at ease. She had been concerned about scratches on the dining room set and the satin cream-colored sofa Father had bought her on their special tenth anniversary.

Moving day finally arrived. It was a sunny Saturday morning. I was up early, washed and dressed and anxious to go to our new home. I put Patches on his leash, took him outside and fastened the end of the leash to the large hook on the side of the garage. He would have shade from the trees and would not be in the way of the moving men going in and out of the house. We had breakfast, Mother and I cleaned up the kitchen, stripped the beds of linens and placed them with the last batch of clothes and kitchenware in a large empty box we had saved for last minute packing. We put a special label on the box and then went outside to sit down on the bench Father had made.

The moving van arrived on time. The men set about their business of loading the truck with our possessions. When the moving men were ready to leave, my parents checked every room and closet to be sure nothing was left behind. Mother and I washed the kitchen and bathroom sinks, swept all the floors and closed and locked all the windows. Father had secured the cellar windows and door, then put Patches two baskets in the rear of the station wagon. I picked up Patches, unfastened his leash from the hook, and climbed into our car. I held Patches all the way to our new home. Father drove slowly so the moving van driver could follow us, and very carefully so he wouldn't spill the pot of coffee and quart of milk Mother had placed in a small pail on the floor between her feet.

As we turned the corner and drove down the street where our new home was located, I had a warm feeling inside me. The house was now in view, it seemed to beckon us on. Father pulled in the driveway up to the garage and we all climbed out. I went out first with Patches, he was getting a little nervous so I put him down on the ground and walked him around the yard. Father had saved a big hook especially for Patches leash. The first thing he did was secure the hook to the side of the garage in about the same area as a hook had been on our old garage. He called me over to him and assured me that Patches would be safe here. I took the cats food dishes and gave Patches some water and food. I sat down on the ground nearby, to watch what was going on, and to stay out of the way.

I watched as the moving van pulled up to the curb. Two men jumped out of the truck and gave directions to the driver about backing up over the curb, up the sidewalk, all the way to the edge of the front porch steps. The men opened the two big doors on the back of the truck and pulled out a long platform. One end they fastened securely to the porch floor and the other end was latched onto the truck. The driver and another man jumped down out of the truck and went into the house with Father. The parade of furniture and boxes being carried from the truck into the house seemed endless. Finally, the truck was empty, the platform was put back inside the van. Father thanked the men for putting all the furniture in place per mothers' instructions and handed the driver an envelope.

I remember exploring the whole house and the entire yard that Saturday afternoon. The rooms were very large and square shaped. The front door opened to a long entrance hall that led clear thru to the big kitchen. There were rows of the cabinets for Mother to put her dishes, pots and pans in. There was a large walk-in pantry for our food storage. The dining room and parlor had large windows and there were two sliding doors that separated the two rooms. I went back to the hall and up the stairs that led to the bedrooms. My parent's bedroom faced the front of the house. There were large double windows in the front and the side of the room and a big closet. My bedroom faced the back of the house with large double windows overlooking a big shade tree. Then there was another bedroom—Mother had said for guests—it had a side view of the yard. There was another door in the upstairs hall. I remember exploring the large attic. At first it seemed spooky, probably because of my young age. The supporting rafters seemed to cast eerie shadows. There were four small windows. Two in the front and two in the back. I remembered the day Father had climbed up on the roof and checked the four gables to be sure there were no repairs needed. Mothers voice came loud and clear—I was needed down stairs—no more exploring for now.

Mother and I had unpacked just enough linen for the beds plus some soap and towels for us to take a bath. I had helped unpack some kitchen boxes while Mother made a big pot of one of her wonderful soups for supper. I set the kitchen table and called Father to come and eat. We had all agreed that soup had really tasted good. After supper I helped clean up the kitchen and then the three of us sat outside on the front porch for a while. Relaxing and just enjoying a cool breeze. That night we went to bed early to get a good night sleep.

Sunday morning, we were up early, had something to eat, then to church. Mother reminded us that we should thank God for our new home. Every Sunday except in very bad weather we went to church. Father and Mother believed one day of the week should be set-aside for the Lord. I grew up with this teaching and as the years passed that belief stayed inside.

Our home was large but had a comfortable feeling about it. Father liked to work around the house. He had enclosed half of the porch with screens he had made on wooden frames and then attached them to the porch ceiling and floor, just inside the big round white columns that supported the porch roof. He surprised Mother with a porch swing he had made for her. We watched as he chains to both sides of the swing and then set the other ends on large hooks that were in the porch ceiling. That swing still hangs on the porch and holds many fond memories for me.

Mother had always loved a garden. She enjoyed spending hours planting, trimming, weeding, watching the plants grow from seedlings to mature flowering scrubs that still continue to bring forth beautiful blooms every year.

I remember watching the big shade tree pop out green buds on all her branches early every spring. The yellow and pink Crocus blooms that brightened our lawn after a long cold winter and then would disappear until the following spring. Those little flowers multiplied every year.

There had always been a border of blooming flowers along the sidewalk leading up to the front steps then around the house following the path to the garage. In the spring Mother had purple Iris, yellow, pink and red Tulips, and purple Hyacinths. When these flowers had finished their term of decorating our yard and had wilted away, Mother would trim them off close to the ground. She would clear the area for the Chrysanthemums to pop up that would grow into little green bushes. The Mums would burst forth with bright yellow, orange and shades of lavender blossoms in late summer. These lasted until the first heavy frost, sometimes even into late December. On bright clear days the sunshine seemed to dance along the blossoms. On dull dreary days, the blossoms brought a smile from anyone passing by, giving a cheerful greeting. They were a delight to see.

I remember helping to plant the Lilac bushes along the sides of the property from the street to the rear edge of our yard. As years drifted by those small Lilac bushes grew to be eight-foot high hedges that flowered profusely each spring. Mother cut Lilac bouquets for the neighbors, my schoolteachers, Aunt Sophie, the local grocer, and anyone else who happened to stop and admire the tall flowering spheres.

Early one spring Saturday morning Father had a surprise for Mother. He had helped a local nursery owner build some hothouses for young plants. As an extra bonus the owner gave us two flowering Dogwood trees. Mother decided that those two trees should be planted in the front yard, one on each side of the walkway. With plenty of loving care they grew quickly and spread budding long limbs that gave shade all summer after the pink blossoms faded.

It seemed to me that we added something new every year. Aunt Sophie even gave a helping hand. She could grow the tallest yellow and red flowering Cannas I had even seen. Of course, Mother was the receiver of twelve of the heartiest Canna plants Aunt Sophie had grown. These were placed across the back yard, in front of the white picket fence that stretched from the garage to the far rear corner of the yard. Every season at the proper time Mother would dig up the bulbous roots and dry them out in the cellar for the following season.

Lying in bed, gazing out at the leafy branches of the hugs shade tree I wondered where Mother had found the time and energy to keep our yard the showplace of the neighborhood. Certainly, I should at least try to keep that part of her spirit alive at OUR HOMESTEAD.

3

YOUTHFUL DAYS

After the weekend move to our new home, Sunday worship service and helping clean up the dinner dishes the three of us had relaxed on the front porch. I remembered that day in particular because it was a special time for family. It made us feel good inside to know we had settled into our new home.

Father pulled his watch out of his pants pocket and remarked that it was eight p.m. Mother reminded me that Monday morning I had to get up early to get ready for school. I excused myself and went inside the house and up the stairs to my room. The chenille pink bathrobe that Aunt Sophie had given me for a Christmas present a year ago was hanging on the clothes hook that was fastened to my bedroom door. I undressed, put on the robe, picked up my nightgown and proceeded down the hall to the big bathroom. After a nice hot bath (which was a nightly ritual) I put on my nightgown and climbed into the bed. Mother and Father came in later and kissed me and said goodnight, as they did every night.

School days seemed to go by so slowly. As I progressed thru grammar school, the work got harder. My parents assured me many times this was to be expected. There was homework every weekday night. They verbally exclaimed their confidence in me quite often, helping me gain

16

my self-confidence to achieve a good education. Days, weeks, months, years passed by, graduation day came and seemed to end too quickly.

The young years had been just great. I had made many friends at school. My closest friends happened to live in our neighborhood. There was Eleanore, a quiet, serious minded person. She had long straight dark hair and dark eyes. Weekdays after school she helped her parents in their small grocery store. They always had a bag of candy or cookies ready to give us. Eleanore loved to read. She was always going to the public library to borrow books, she liked mysteries best. We all were very surprised when she announced, after graduation, that she was going to college and planned on becoming a history teacher.

Mamie lived three houses down the street from me. She had shoulder length blonde hair that hung in a pageboy style. Her older sisters were already working full time so Mamie had been put in charge of her younger brother. She was always helping with the housework. I remember how she scrubbed the kitchen floor and then would lay newspapers down to make a path to walk on. Once a month on a Saturday morning, she would place a ladder under their kitchen window. With a pail of ammonia water and old newspapers she would commence cleaning all the windows. Mamie wasn't the studious type, more like a homemaker. Her mother taught her how to cook and prepare special recipes that had been handed down thru the generations. Her cuisine knowledge and expertise were generously shared with her friends. Mamie was and still is my closest, very dearest friend.

Trudy was a slender tall blonde. Her hair was short and curly. She had matured early and had the best figure of all the girls in school. She had been voted the most popular three years in a row. She had two older sisters and one younger sister. Trudy had a special knack of being serious about her schoolwork yet was able to project a sense of humor. Her two older sisters owned a dress shop in town and as soon as Trudy was old enough, she went to work for them part-time. That was the reason she was always voted the best dressed.

The four of us really enjoyed every minute that we had together. There were picnics with our families. Our parents would always invite all of us when one of them planned an outing. Of course, we were called the "camp fire girls". We would gather the kindling, leaves, wood and help get the fire started. We always made sure there were four long sturdy sticks set aside. These were shaved to a point on one end to hold a hotdog, apple, or marshmallows that were held over the fire until they were almost charcoal. We were also in charge of putting out the fire and making sure no hot ashes were left to start up again. We were all taught love and respect for the outdoors and the little creatures of the woods.

The four of us went thru scouting together. Earning our badges as we went from Brownies thru Girl Scouts. There were field trips we had taken, rain or shine, that will always be remembered. Christmas presents we made for our parents that were used until they gave out with age, then probably were packed away for safekeeping and memories.

In the summer besides picnics we went to the circus. There would be large colorful posters tacked on poles all around town. The circus always arrived on a Friday for the parade and to set up their tents. There were two performances on Saturday and Sunday. There was always the big parade thru the main street. It would start with clowns in colorful costumes and funny painted faces, followed by the ringmaster and all the performers in horse driven wagons. Then came the wild animal cages, a colorful wagon train, some very large elephants followed by some more clowns. My parents always bought tickets for both days. We would take Aunt Sophie one day and my friends were treated for the second trip. During the circus performance boys dressed in candy striped uniforms and carrying large trays loaded with peanuts, popcorn, soda and cotton candy, would walk around the rows of the bleacher seats selling their wares, until they were sold out. The circus people would work all Sunday night packing up and, by Monday morning they were gone, leaving the grounds clean and raked.

Then there was the amusement park. The four of us always saved our allowances all year for this special treat. We all had local babysitting jobs in our early teen years up until we graduated. The money we earned was added to our allowances. This enabled us to go to the amusement park once a week all summer long. There were slow rides like the merry-go-round and ferries wheel and individual two-seater airplanes hung on long chains that were suspended from a center post high above. The planes would swing outward in a circle as the motor in the center post was started. The fast rides like the whip, tilt-a-whirl, caterpillar, octopus and chair swing were our favorites. The huge roller coaster was a ride the four of us had tried early one season. We all agreed once was enough, but every year we went back on the roller coaster again. There was a ten-piece band led by a stout white haired mistro in a blue and white uniform. He led the entertaining band twice a day. The band stand was surrounded by long picnic tables and framed by booths where you could buy hotdog, hamburgers, soda, beer and of course those delicious French fries. The aroma of many different hot pans of food filled the air—there was no need to bring your own picnic basket. After the band played for an hour, they would pack up their music and instruments and head for the circus area. The circus had high wire acts, jugglers, animal acts and much more. Every act was accompanied by the band music. You could see this entertainment in the afternoons and evenings. Along the path to the circus area there was a spook house, the house of mirrors, stands of chance with large spinning wheels, a dunk-the-clown in a large tub of water game and some I have forgotten. What pleasant memories those days bring back to me.

In the fall our Girl Scout Troop and the church sponsored hayrides that gave my friends and I a lot of fun filled hours. We made sure not to miss one of them. The wagon over-loaded with hay and driven by a kindly old gentleman led the two large horses out of town and along the dirt road that led to a big farm. All the way the horse driver would lead the group in songs. He took the wagon up to the front gate, up the path to the big red farmhouse where a sweet old lady would greet us with hot chocolate and homemade cookies. The hayride back home was always a laughing, singing, happy ride combined with just a little bit of mischief.

As the weather turned cold our spirits again perked up with the thought of the coming winter season that would hopefully bring plenty of snow. Father had made a sleigh that was long, low to the ground with metal tracks he had fastened tightly. They had just enough curve upward at the front tips. Every fall he would take the sleigh off the garage wall hooks, sharpen, clean and polish the tracks for me. After the first heavy snowfall had been packed down on the streets by cars riding by, I would take my sleigh around the corner and up the street to the top of the small hill. When no cars were in sight I would run with my sleigh and do a belly flop all the way down, as a trial run. My friends and I would then walk with our sleighs to the nearby park. There was big hill that swept up and down and up and down again. That was the favorite spot for sleighing. It was always crowded with the town youngers and their sleighs and sauces. Of course, some of us had a few tumbles but nothing serious.

Our next winter sport was ice-skating on the large park pond. We waited anxiously each winter for the park ranger to check the ice for thickness and safety. When the all-clear decision was made the word spread like wildfire. We would hurry home to tell our folks and to search thru our closet for the ice skates. Mother had given me a pair every couple of years. As I grew out of one pair, they were donated to someone who couldn't afford to buy skates. Although my balance was bad, I still loved wobbling around the pond. It was exciting trying to keep my balance and yet look relaxed. I would daydream of becoming a champion figure skater—that dream came to an abrupt end when I slipped and fell into a nearby snow bank.

During the high school years, the four of us remained close. We gave up sleighing, and ice-skating for roller-skating. Weekdays were always filled with our education but on Saturdays we had our time of fun. Sometimes we went roller-skating or to the movies or just lounged around one another's home talking of our future.

My parents love and deep understanding of all my needs and problems, whether large or small, was combined with a strong yet gentle touch of discipline.

My friends and I graduated and went on to our chosen careers. They married later on while I chose to stay single. That was the conclusion of our YOUTHFUL DAYS.

4

CAREER YEARS

After graduation I began the task of filing applications for employment at the large department store and the medical building complex. There was a part time opening in the loungerie area of the department store. I accepted the position and after a few weeks was put on full time. I was always on time for work and anxious to learn. As time passed, I was taught all about selling, pricing, different materials and with some coaching I was trained to order the merchandise.

From that time on my self-confidence grew. I left the department store for a job as medical secretary in a work pool at the medical complex. It was a on-the-job training program. Hours were long and my weekends disrupted by staggered work shifts. Time passed without advancement, so I began the task of looking for another job.

Over the years our little quiet town had explained and grown into a bustling, busy city without disturbing the quiet beauty of the suburbs.

I filed papers for employment at the local bank. My application was reviewed by the manager. His secretary phoned out house early one Monday morning and informed me of a date set for my interview. Mr. Jones had remembered my name from years ago when my parents applied for their home loan. Mr. Jones read aloud my application then

22

proceeded to question my plans for the future. Excusing himself he took my papers and went into the personnel office. I sat anxiously awaiting his final determination. When Mr. Jones returned, he had a smile on his face. I had passed the interview with flying colors and was given the opportunity to enter the banking system.

I was hired as a secretary and later on sent to school to be trained as a bank teller. As time passed, I was promoted to Assistant Manager of the bank.

For the past twenty years I had followed orders, as clerk and then Assistant Manager. I had always done my best to be pleasant to everyone, while doing each daily assignment with thorough completion. Now my career life would change. I was to be the one who was in charge, making decisions that affected people's lives in a financial way. My new position gave me authority over the employees, final decision on all loans and much more. It would also give me plenty of headaches to go along with the complex problems of banking.

I accepted the promotion and huge responsibility. After all, I was trained for banking, this was my career. The thought of my parents growing older, needing help someday, and I as the only child also played a part in my decision.

For the next ten years I applied what knowledge I already possessed and added extra banking courses to it. As a manager my decisions had been made from rules, experience and intuition.

The economy had turned upwards. The banking business prospered with the growth of our town that became a busy metropolis. I felt proud knowing that I had helped indirectly. The bank president, together with the first vice president and board of directors, had decided to enlarge our facilities.

With the retirement of the bank president shortly thereafter the vice president moved up to president. I was now in a financial position, and station in life, to plan for my parents a life of leisure and luxury for their later years, which were approaching all too soon.

I graciously accepted my new position as vice president of our bank. This was to be the height of my CAREER YEARS.

5

LEISURE TIME

Thru the years Mother spent her space time on two hobbies—gardening and crocheting. When there was a lull in weeding and pruning, she would start crocheting in alfghan with one of her favorite patterns. She had made them for our beds, the couch in the parlor, Aunt Sophie, her nieces, my friends, and the church bazaar. Mother would always say this was her way of relaxing.

Later, in life she began to slow down. The garden flourished with my help. The blooms were as bright and numerous as ever. Mother spent more time on crocheting and helping on projects for the women's club of our church.

There are recipes in Mother's kitchen files that are a combination of family favorites, originals from friends, relatives and neighbors. On weekends, when I have the urge, I thumb thru the numerous card file and pick out one of my favorites. Mother had a special culinary touch that made the taste buds wake up. I never could get the same taste. Some favorites of mine are her homemade cup custard, bread pudding, roast duck with orange glaze sauce and those delicious dumplings to go with the pot roast.

While Mother busied herself inside the house, Father spent his spare time in his cellar workshop. From the time I was small I could remember Father making something out of a piece of wood. There were birdhouses that hung from our large shade tree, every year they were the birthplace of chirping feathered friends. There still stands the flower trellis Mother wanted. One Christmas he surprised me with a two-story dollhouse complete with a fireplace and chimney. The sleigh that gave me many hours of fun hangs on the cellar wall, unlike the porch swing that will never outgrow it's usefulness. Father had made his workbenches, a picnic table and benches. He always saved some scraps of wood that were fashioned into flowerpots or toy airplanes for the neighborhood kids. I think one of his pet projects was the kite he made of wood and paper and then would fasten long long tails of scrap material on one end. He made my toy chest, and later on the large blanket chest, and the window seat that Mother padded with some foam and then covered it with a crocheted alfghan. It fit under the double window in my bedroom like a glove, and still remains one of my favorite places to sit and enjoy the view of our garden.

One Friday evening in the fall, after dinner, Father announced that he was going to retire from the railroad. After fifty years of service he was able to receive a monthly pension. He had figured out how much our expenses were and what would be left after each month's bills. Mother was taken by surprise but agreed it was time to retire. There were savings accounts that would help to keep them financially stable. The company gave Father a retirement dinner and a gold watch, the big day was over, and now he would have plenty of leisure time to start a few more hobbies or just relax in his easy chair.

Mother had suggested that they take a few trips to see parts of the country which Father heartily agreed too. He got a map of the United States out of his big roll top desk, (that was our present to him many years ago), spread it out on the dining room table and called to us to join him. He said we should each choose three states. Mother picked

Pennsylvania, Virginia and Florida. Father picked New York, Maine and Vermont. I chose California, Texas and New Mexico.

They were blessed with good health. For the next few years they traveled by bus car, plane and train. Each time they returned home their arms were full of souvenirs and picture post cards. I would sit and listen as they went into great detail about their experiences.

One summer Father surprised Mother with trip back to Niagara Falls, Canada. That was their honeymoon destination when they were first married. Of course, Mother was delighted. The weather had been perfect and I remember her exclaiming that the falls ang gardens were as beautiful as ever.

Time went by quickly after that season. A few years passed. Mother became weaker and grew tired early in the day. With much persuasion she had gone to her doctor for a checkup. Within one moth she was gone. Father grieved for her so intensely that he couldn't eat or sleep. One evening as he settled into his easy chair, I busied myself in the kitchen. I called but he did not answer. I dried my hands on the kitchen towel and went inside. There he sat—looking so relaxed. The reality of his passing on struck me hard. That winter I grieved for both my parents.

The all too vivid memories of the past have put me in an almost stupefied trance. I lie here in bed realizing that the past will always haunt me in a very pleasant way. I am the sole heir of a grand old house. A homestead full of wonderful memories of a past never to be forgotten.

Now I am the one who will enjoy life's LEISURE TIME.

6

DECISION DAY

Monday mornings seemed to arrive too quickly in the past six months. My weekends were used trying to keep the old homestead clean and shiny, and hours were spent on gardening. This left little time for relaxing. So many times, I had planned to take a short trip but just couldn't fit it into my weekend schedule.

I had my usual breakfast of juice, cereal and coffee, cleaned the kitchen table, washed, dried and put away the dishes. I went upstairs, took my morning shower, got dressed picked up my briefcase, purse and car keys, made sure the windows and doors were locked, then proceeded down the porch steps to my car. The air was cool and crisp. Autumn had come upon this part of the country very early. The trees lining the street were beginning to put on their annual splender of colors, rich yellow, orange and red leaves waved in the breeze. The mums that lined the sidewalk were already bursting into blooms. After starting my car and backing out of the driveway I realized how chilly I felt, the car heater was turned on. Oh, now that felt much better. The drive to town was a short one. I parked in my reserved spot in the bank parking lot, locked the car and proceeded into the bank.

Once inside my office I settled down at my desk for another day of banking business. By noontime I had three meetings scheduled for

28

me for the afternoon. I poured myself a cup of coffee then sat back to relax for a few minutes. Most of the bank officers had left the building to attend a fiftieth birthday party for one of the employees. I had excused myself from attending due to the fact that I was on a strict diet—orders from my doctor. Over the years the calories had turned into pounds.

Sitting back in my chair a sudden thought struck me. Maybe I should retire. The more I tried to brush the thought away, the more it persisted. Here I was, a vice president of our local bank, loving the work I did, enjoying my fellow employees. Every workday filled with interesting people, some days routine, some days holding a challenge. The more it became a very feasible idea. After all, there were very competent younger officers to choose from to take my place. Certainly, this fine old bank that was established long ago had conducted profitable business without my help and would continue to do so for many years to come after I left. Well that was that! I would retire! There was plenty of things that I could do to occupy my free time. For the next few minutes I sat at my desk listing everything I would like to do and never before had the time. That list became quite large.

Lunchtime was over, the partygoers were returning to their desks. By one p.m. everyone was back to their routine, business was moving along smoothly as usual. My secretary had obtained an appointment for me to meet with the bank president at two p.m. The hour went quickly as I went thru the last of my paperwork for the day. My signature was put on a home loan I had approved previously. The couple had applied for a mortgage on one of the fine older homes in our town. They had a ten-year-old daughter who accompanied them during meetings. For a moment, a brief moment, she had reminded me of myself, a day with my parents that happened long, long ago.

At precisely two p.m. I went into Mr. Fisher's office. He asked me to sit down and explain what the problem was. I assured him that there was no problem. As a matter of fact—this had been a very pleasant day. I explained that my decision to retire was definite and I would not change my mind. There was a folder on my desk with the names of a few very qualified and competent officers that I would recommend for my job. The bank president sat there in astonishment. He remarked that someday he knew I would retire but this really caught him by surprise. After a lengthy conversation, Mr. Fisher agreed with me that the time was right to retire. He wished me well and assured me of my pension amount and medical policies that I was entitled to. I thanked him and returned to my office.

The next two weeks were filled with training a new vice president to take my place. That last day of work I was given a retirement luncheon. It was wonderful joyous yet sad time for me. There were gifts I would treasure forever, including the gold watch engraved with my name and date of retirement. It was a policy of the bank to give the desk and chair, of the officer retiring, as a gift. After the luncheon, I picked up my personal belongings along with my gold engraved briefcase, said my goodbyes and left. The two maintenance men loaded my desk and chair into their truck and followed me home. I had made a special place for the desk in the large living room. It would sit in a corner by the window that overlooked the side yard and those huge flowering Lilac bushes.

That Monday two weeks ago had been my DECISION DAY.

7

FAMILY REUNION

The following weeks were spent just relaxing around the house. It was nice to be able to lay in bed mornings, not having to get up with the alarm clock, especially on those cold rainy damp fall days. My goodness, I never realized how much I would really enjoy this type of life. No more rush to get showered, eat in a hurry and then drive thru early morning traffic to a job (career) I really had enjoyed but one that had plenty of responsibility and problems. Then the drive home in rain, sleet, snow or shine, thru hectic traffic and sometimes-perilous weather conditions. Pulling the pink soft satin covered quilt a little higher and tucking my arms under, I thought on, in a convincing manner, this retirement life was going to be just great.

The fall air was getting cooler; Thanksgiving Day was just one month away. Wondering what to do and which one of my relatives would call to invite me, I decided to turn-the-table this year, and call all of them. Yes! That was it! I would have the Thanksgiving Day dinner and invite my three nieces and my nephew and their families. The first item on the agenda was to call the family.

I dialed Mary's number. She was the oldest. Mary and Joe had been very busy lately renovating a cape-cod style home they had purchased in South Jersey. In the past two years they had painted the entire house

31

inside and out. Installed an in-ground swimming pool and now were in the mist of finishing the cellar that had been turned into a rumpus room with a petition for a workshop for Joe. With all that renovation he certainly needed a workshop. A place where he could keep the many tools and yet not have them scattered all over the house—as Mary had put it. Their two children were nine and seven years old. Little Joe had a paper route, while his little sister was too young to be interested in anything but dolls and toys. Besides Joe's regular job he had gone into partnership with a friend on a small liquor store. So, every weekend he was in the store. Mary filled her weekend hours by baking, painting, or in the summer by enjoying their in-ground pool. I must say, I also enjoyed it. I was able to tear myself away from my own weekend chores a few times during the season and just relax in the sun after taking a quick dip in the pool. Mary and I had always ended the weekend with a barbecue. Mary answered the phone and called to Joe to pick up the extension in his workshop. They were surprised to hear what I planned and, yes, they were delighted and would be at my house early in the morning to help. Of course, they would stay in the guest room for the weekend and the children would bring their sleeping bags.

Next call was to Sue. Her and Jack also lived in South Jersey. They had three children, two boys and a girl. Jack had been more fortunate with his career. After finishing a tour with the Marines as an honor guard for the President of the United States, in Washington D.C., he returned to civilian life. Jack had a college degree in chemical engineering. After a short vacation with Sue in the islands he was ready to search out his career. The resume Jack submitted to three large corporate headquarters had proved very fruitful. He was accepted by all three companies. Jack chose the one he thought would hold the best future for him and he was right. He now held a position in the chemical department of the corporation. Their home was a lovely split-level on a corner lot surrounded by numerous shade trees. Their attached garage held one car and many bikes and weight lifting equipment. The motor home they had purchased a few years ago was kept on the far side of the house. Jacks jalopy as he called it was kept parked in the driveway. That old car Jack used to go back and forth to work every day – while Sue used the new sedan for her shopping sprees. Jack had added wood beams and one cedar wall in the living room for decoration, but with a new home there really wasn't too much to do. Jack answered the phone because Sue had a case of laryngitis and couldn't talk (or yell at the kids—to their delight). He relayed my invitation to Sue and he told me that she shook her head yes—that was fine with him also. They would bring their motor home and stay in there for the weekend. The kids could bring their sleeping bags and park themselves in the living room.

Sally's home was only two miles away from me. Her and Jim had one son, Jim Jr., he was a delight to talk to. For all of his six years of age he spoke in a very grown up manner, and his diction was clear and punctuated. Amazing when I think of it. Sally and Jim put all their money into income properties. He was a real go-getter. The fishing boat had enabled them to live vary comfortably and yet invest in three duplexes. While Jim went out commercial fishing for three and four days at a time, Sally took charge collecting rents, taking care of minor problems and repairs and on top of that, keeping her own house in top shape, and taking Jim Jr. back and forth to school. I often wondered where one found all that time and energy. A few years ago, they had the opportunity to buy a house and directly across the street from the duplexes. After a coat of paint, some new awnings and a fence around the property to help Sally keep tabs on little Jim. The house became a lovely, attractive home. Sally had even found time to plant some flowers. I rang her number— no answer – so I called later in the day. Sally was delighted with my invitation. She would tell Jim about it when he returned from his fishing trip. Sally suggested that she help me shop or maybe bake something. I thanked her and said that we would get together next week.

The last call was to Larry. He was my only nephew. Larry and Debbie and their two children lived in a rural area of New Jersey that had recently been developed. A lovely quiet area nestled in the countryside, about ten miles from town, with a high elevation and a beautiful view of the river. The entire community Is surrounded by acres of trees that had been left untouched by man, to grow tall reaching up their limbs to touch the sky, to breathe the clean clear air. Larry had always loved working out with weights when he wasn't playing football or running. As a result, his body was as Debbie had said "hard as steel". He could lift her up with one arm. Larry had signed up with the Air Force, and was made an A.P. (air force police). When his tour was up, he and Debbie married. He tried a few different jobs and discovered he was great at selling. So, after working for some small companies he was offered a chance to sell for a large company. He soon was made manager of the home plant and now is a district manager. While Larry is away from home, Debbie fills the hours with trying new recipes, taking the children back and forth to school and doing some sewing. I dialed their number. Debbie answered and after hearing my idea, she too was delighted. She would bring the children—but Larry may have to be out of town. There was a big deal cooking upstate and knowing Larry—he wasn't going to miss out on possibly obtaining a very large account. Debbie said she would bake some pies and the children would gather some pinecones and brown leaves for table decorations.

Well now! That was taken care of. I made a list for the menu and a seating arrangement. Of course, a large turkey—better count my list of hungry eaters. Joe, Mary and their two children. Sue, Jack and their three children. Sally, Jim and Jim Jr. Larry, Debbie and their two children. That made sixteen plus me.

Goodness gracious! I hadn't realized, where would I seat seventeen people? I decided I would move the dining room table over to the sidewall near the kitchen and rent two long tables with folding chairs from our local lodge. The dining table could be used as a serving table. For that weekend I would serve buffet style. I made a list of food items I needed including wine and beer to serve with the meal and soda for the children. I had plenty of dinnerware and sets of silverware and glassware I had collected over the years.

The following week I called Sally and she and I went shopping while Jim Jr. was in school. There was the huge turkey, yams, marshmallows, cranberry sauce, turnip, celery, cream cheese, nuts, crackers, olives, bread, candies, beverages, extra coffee and tea, sugar, spices, carrots, and cauliflower. Butter, milk, eggs, bacon and a few other perishables I could buy last minute. After Sally helped me carry the grocery bags into the kitchen, she left to pick up Jim Jr. at school. I put the groceries away and then sat down to relax with a cup of tea while I made a list of items I still needed. I rewrote my menu for the big day and figured out what I would make for the weekend for Mary and Sue and their families. By the time I was finished with my lists it was five thirty p.m. I decided to go into town to the café restaurant for dinner, then go to a movie.

Thanksgiving Day was here. I woke up early to watch the sun rise. It was going to be a beautiful clear day. The temperature had warmed a few degrees which would really make the day pleasant. I showered, dressed, put my apron on and went downstairs to the kitchen. After breakfast I cleared the dishes away and brought the turkey out to be cleaned and washed. Just as I started there was a knock on the front door. It was Sally bright and early as she had promised. She had left Jim Jr. with a neighbor. Jim had went fishing but would be back in time for dinner. She presented me with a large paper bag. Inside were fresh clams and oysters and six lovely sized lobsters. Sally made me promise to save the lobsters for myself as a special treat. I put a large pot of water on to boil, added salt and mustard and put the lobsters in the pot to cook until I made room in the freezer for them. I carefully wrapped each one separately, placed a label on each package and put them in the freezer.

Now to prepare the clams and oysters. We washed the shells, cracked them open and decided to make Clams Casino and Oyster Rockafeller as appetizers. After preparations were done, they were placed on trays covered and put into the refrigerator. Just before dinner I would put them into the microwave oven that had been a present from my nephew Larry last Christmas.

Sally peeled and cut up the vegetables while I washed the huge turkey inside and out with salt water. I put the turkey on paper towels to dry off while I made the stuffing. My Mother had a special recipe that she had taught me to use many years ago and I made sure that this and all the other recipes were passed along to my nieces and nephew. Larry was a practicing chef in his spare time when he was home with the family. When the stuffing was ready, Sally held the turkey as I stuffed and then tied the ends together to hold all that goodness inside. After the turkey went into the oven I put on a pot of coffee for Sally and me. We talked about her family while preparing the celery and cream cheese snacks.

The front door bell rang. Mary, Joe and the children were here, followed by Sue, Jack and their family. Mary placed the two gallons of cider they brought on the kitchen table. Sue put the apple and pumpkin pies she had baked on the dining room table. The children went outside to play while Mary and Sue busied themselves setting the tables. Joe and Jack mixed a beverage and went out on the porch to review the worldly situation—I guess.

Larry and Debbie arrived with their children each carrying a pie— we surely were going to have enough good desserts. Larry did not have to go out of town after all. Larry joined Joe and Jack on the porch while Debbie grabbed an apron and began helping to clean up the kitchen. I checked the refrigerator to be sure there was enough soda for the children—thank goodness—there was plenty. Then I took the cream out of the freezer to thaw. After all, what is pie without whipped topping? The vegetables were put on to cook; nuts and fruit were placed on the table. While the girls were having chitchat, I arranged a centerpiece for the dining room table, some fall leaves, nuts and a little ceramic turkey I had purchased at my friend's specialty shop. Then the candles in their little ceramic pilgrim holders were placed inside the circle of leaves. I returned to the kitchen, removed the vegetables from the stove, took off my apron and joined Mary, Sue and Sally, the four of us took a stroll around the yard. I called to the children and asked them to pick a nice bouquet of mums that we could put on the side table in one of my favorite vases. By the time the children were thru picking flowers, there were enough blossoms to fill three vases. But no matter, this was a festive holiday season and the many extra flowers would brighten up the other rooms.

Sally left to pick up Jim Jr., when she returned to my delight, Jim was with them. He had come in early with a boatload of fish. He had taken the time to fillet a large pan full of Flounder that he knew I could make good use of on the weekend. I must tell you; Jim has always been this thoughtful of others.

The turkey was just about done, the girls wanted to help in the kitchen but I lovingly chased them out—they had helped enough and after all—I was the hostess today. I made the gravy, warmed the vegetables, put two pots of the coffee on, and removed the clam and oysters from the refrigerator and placed them in the microwave oven. After a few minutes they were done to perfection. I immediately put them on little dishes and placed them on the long tables at each individual setting. The vegetables I put in the antique tourines that were my Mothers—her gravy boat was filled to the brim. I removed the stuffing and placed it on one of the platters. After all the foods were on the table, I called everyone into the house. When they were all seated, I brought out the turkey on my Mother's antique platter and placed it in front of my nephew. Mary lit the candles and brought a bucket of ice cubes out of the kitchen. Sally poured the soda and cider. I gave the blessing to out table of food, then

Lary proceeded to carve the big bird. For the next few hours' plates were passed and everyone feasted. When it was obvious no more dinner could be consumed, Sue helped clear the table of dishes and silverware while I cut the pies and passed out the pie plates. Of course, the children wanted the whipped cream on their piece of pie, with a second glass of soda. It was a good thing I had made extra ice cubes and stored them in the freezer. The children went back outside to the porch. The men took a walk while we girls cleaned up. Debbie replaced the disposable tablecloth with a new one and set the centerpiece in place again. The children came back inside and spread themselves out on the living room floor to watch television. I brought out the family picture albums. I had kept them up-to-date. Picture taking was one of my hobbies. My nieces really had a good time going thru the many pages of pictures with the individual annotations including dates and names of people and places.

Joe, Jack, Larry and Jim came into the room and sat down at the table. They said they had looked the place over inside and out. There were some repairs needed and some painting should be done. It would be their pleasure to do whatever had to be done and whatever else I would like them to do. I was pleasantly shocked. What with working at the bank until my recent retirement and some gardening, I hadn't realized or really checked the house thoroughly, for work needed to be done. I agreed. Anytime that was good with them would be fine with me, but I insisted I pay for all the materials.

By this time all my grandnieces and grandnephews were ready for bed. Mary's and Sue's children took their sleeping bags upstairs. I said they could sleep in my room. Now Debbie's children and Jim Jr. pleaded to stay overnight too. Their parents and I gave in to their pleadings. Debbie and Sue helped make up the roll away beds that were kept stored in the attic. The children were settled down for the night. Larry, Debbie, Sally and Jim left for home. They all would be back tomorrow afternoon. Mary and Joe retired to the spare bedroom. Sue and Jack went to their motor home for the night and I had to admit the fact that I was tired too. I put out all the lights except for a night-light to the kitchen and one in the bathroom, changed into my nightgown, tiptoed between the sleeping bags and climbed into bed stretching out between those stain sheets and pulled the goose down quilt up to my chin. It sure felt good to relax. What a wonderful Thanksgiving Day it had been. Everything had been perfect, including the weather. The whole family was able to be present. I was really pleased with myself that the dinner had turned out to be such a success. With these thoughts I drifted off into a deep sleep.

The rest of the holiday weekend I spent enjoying my grandnieces and grandnephews—they sure can ask a lot of questions. Between meals, televisions, walks around the block and playing games, they all kept quite busy. I wondered where all that energy came from. Debbie and Sally returned to pick up their children and thank me for a wonderful time. Sunday afternoon I prepared a large buffet style dinner for all of us. After filling ourselves with goodies, we sat around for a while just making small talk. Time was getting on; the holiday weekend was over. After many hugs and kisses, Mary, Joe, Sue, Jack, and their families were on their way back home. It was seven p.m. and they would safely miss the heavy traffic. I waved goodbye, closed up the house and settled back in my lounge chair to watch television. The house sure was quiet now. This had been a wonderful happy FAMILY REUNION.

8

TRAVEL JOY and SORROW

Winter weather was coming our way. For the past couple of weeks, the television weatherman was warning the viewers of a huge storm that had stalled out west, but would work its way into our area. The storm was now only two days away and threatening to dump heavy snow on our eastern seaboard states.

I made a trip into town to the travel bureau and inquired about plane reservations to Florida. Mrs. Smith, the travel agent put the information on the computer and it came back with an affirmative answer. I would leave out of Newark Airport on Sunshine Airline Number 1. At eight a.m., Wednesday morning. I would stay at the Sunshine Sea Air Motel. She wrote out my ticket and included the round-trip transportation to the airport and back. Yes, the van would pick me up at my house. I hesitated a few moments, then I decided to take the trip. After all, I was retired now—why should I stay home? Why should I put up with the cold, snowy, icy winter weather? Financially I could afford to travel and maybe I should start travelling while I physically can. That was that. I definitely knew this decision was right'. I picked up my tickets, paid for them with one of my credit cards, thanked Mrs. Smith for her help and left the travel bureau feeling quite happy. My first trip to Florida was going to be a lot of fun.

On the way home I stopped at the department store. Browsing thru women's department, I bought some travelling clothes. The store was now stocked with winter clothes. I would have plenty of time to shop in the malls in Florida. I paid for my purchase and left. Oh! That cold wind was getting stronger and the sky was clouding up. I put the car heater on while driving home. Now that felt much better. I drove the car into the garage. Picked up my packages, locked the garage doors and went inside. After enjoying a hot cup of tea, I called my nieces Debbie to explain my plans. They were all very surprised but very happy for me that I was able to get away for the winter season. Of course, they all lovingly were jealous that they all would have to suffer out the cold stormy winter. No—I didn't need a ride to the airport, the van was going to pick me up. Yes—I had plenty of luggage. I gave them all the information on the airline, time of departure, and the name of the motel I would be staying in. They made me promise to call collect when I arrived. Sally lived the closest to my house, so her and Jim would check it out every week and keep the heat on fifty degrees so the pipes would not freeze. They would be over to pick up the keys and help me pack. I assured them I didn't need help packing but would Sally please empty the refrigerator and take all the foodstuffs home with her. She was welcome to use whatever was in the pantry also. With that taken care of, I settled back in my lounge chair with a pad and pencil and another cup of tea. Now let's see—I would take a few slack sets, two sweaters, some shoes, lingerie, three dresses and a small clutch handbag.

The next morning after breakfast I stripped the linens and made my bed. I brought out the two suitcases and overnight bag and began packing. I carried them down the stairs and set them by the front door. Next, I ran the vacuum and dusted the furniture. After Lunch I went to the post office—they would hold my mail in a rental box and my niece Sally would pick it up when she had the time. Next was a stop at the bank. The teller transferred some of my funds into traveler's checks. She explained, once I was settled in Florida, I could open a checking account and my bank would transfer money down to the Florida bank any time I called to request it using a special code number that only I and the bank knew. When I returned home, I called Sally. She came over and I told her about the post office and bank number. In case of emergency she could transact my business. After Sally left, I put my traveler's checks, tickets and money in my purse and placed the purse on top of the luggage. It was dinnertime and I decided to use the last lobster left in my freezer. Some salad, a baked potato and warmed lobster were a real treat.

The next morning, I woke early, showered, dressed, locked all the windows, back door and waited for the taxi. It arrived right on time. The driver helped me put the luggage in the van, I took a seat and with a last lingering glance at the homestead as we drove away. The ride to the airport was hectic. Traffic was heavy on a weekday morning. Snow was starting to fall. It was a light dry snow that blew sideways with the wind. By the time we reached the airport the snow had turned heavy and was beginning to stick to the ground. I stepped out of the van and slipped on some snow. I almost fell but one of the baggage clerks caught me. I thanked him and proceeded into the terminal. My luggage was placed on the conveyor belt while the clerk checked my ticket. There was still half hour to departure time so I put the ticket back in my purse and walked over to the coffee shop. It was cafeteria style, the waiting line was short, and as I moved up in line the aroma of hot cinnamon buns tickled my nostrils. The girl poured a cup of coffee and placed a bun on my tray with a napkin. No—I didn't want anything else. I paid the cashier and found a small table against the side wall. The bun and coffee were just enough to satisfy my nervous stomach.

The clock on the terminal wall read seven forty-five a.m., so I picked up my purse, freshened my lipstick and walked thru the terminal to the correct departure gate, then thru the airport security check point. There was a very long line of people waiting to board the plane. I was last on the line. Thank goodness my seat was already reserved. The stewardesses were smiling as they ushered the passengers to their seats. Once the carryon luggage was secured, pillows handed out, and a demonstration given by the stewardesses, of the life support system, we were requested to fasten our seatbelts. I glanced out the small window but my view was obscured by the blowing snow. The captain assured us via the loudspeaker system that everything was under control, the tower had given an all clear to proceed down the runway for takeoff. The stewardesses checked everyone's seatbelt then settled themselves down with assurance for the takeoff.

I thought to myself how amazing it was that a plane so huge and heavy could actually lift off the ground and fly. The plane taxied across the airstrip, paused at the far end then picked up speed as we sped down the runway, then the plane started to lift off the ground. It climbed at a steep angle then made a half turn and seemed to just glide, slicing thru the snow and cloud layers until we were above the clouds. What a beautiful shade of blue the sky was, it looked so clear and serene. The clouds looked like mountains of puffy white cotton, so soft they could be formed into any shape, I was glad I had a window seat. For the next few minutes I held my little camera up to the window, taking pictures of the cloud formations. One looked like an angel's wing, another a mushroom, one even resembled a dog head complete with the big square nose and big ears.

The all-clear light came on above the doorway. The captain announced the planes airspeed, how high we were flying, weather conditions and what city and state we were flying over. The stewardess assured us we no longer needed the seat belts buckled. I could hear glasses clinking at the far end of our compartment, I glanced around to see a cocktail cart coming our way. The stewardess looked quite adept, as she served the soda, cocktails and made change. Now it was my turn. Yes, I would like a vodka and orange. She handed me a plastic glass filled with orange juice and a miniature bottle of vodka. The gentleman sitting next to me insisted on paying for both our drinks. I thanked him then proceeded to try and open that little bottle. My! That bottle top was really secure! The gentleman chuckled and then took the bottle out of my hand and with one quick little turn he had it opened. He poured the contents into my glass of juice and handed the empty bottle back to me. Yes—I agreed it would make a cute souvenir. The man introduced himself as Mr. Brent Bowen and said he was a retired fireman from New York and that he was planning on staying in Florida for the entire winter season. His inquisitive glance told me it was my turn to talk. My retirement as a vice president of our local bank had now given me time also to spend the winter months in Florida. After exchanging conversation back and forth, we acknowledged the fact that both of us were single. He had always thought his life as a fireman was to hectic and dangerous to involve a family in. Then Mr. Bowen asked if he could take me out to dinner sometime. I thought a minute the answered "yes". I would enjoy that. I gave Mr. Bowen my address that I would be staying at while in Florida. Just as I settled back and closed my eyes to rest the stewardess came down the isle with our dinner trays. How inventive this little tray was, just the right size to fit on the tray that protruded from the rear of the seat in front of me. With indentations for a cup, plate and desert dish. The sealed package of three pieces of silverware and napkin also contained packets of sugar, salt and pepper. My watch read nine thirty a.m. We were due to land at ten thirty a.m. in Fort Lauderdale. No wonder I felt hungry, the only breakfast I had was the coffee and bun in the airport terminal. I buttered my toast, cut the sausages, salted the eggs and creamed the coffee. After finishing breakfast Mr. Bowen took the empty trays back to the kitchenette and returned to his seat. For the next half hour, I just relaxed with my eyes closed.

At precisely ten thirty a.m. the "fasten seatbelt" light came on, the stewardess walked down the aisle checking everyone's seatbelt and making sure the trays and seats were in an upright position. I glanced out the window, the sun was shining and the sky was a clear light blue. I looked down, we were over the ocean, I could see the outline of the Florida coastline. As the plane started a downward glide, the high condominiums, fishing pier that jutted out quite a distance into the ocean to our left, and some pine trees were now distinguishable. The plane passed over a highway then lowered until its wheels touched the runway. It raced along the ground, slowing down then came to a complete stop at the far end of the runway. It seemed forever until the pilot taxied the plane around to the proper airport terminal. When we came to a complete stop, there was an empty pleated form coming toward the plane from the terminal. It resembled the center of an accordion—the part that is squeezed together to make the sounds, but moving slow as a caterpillar does, creeping along, then bumping its nose against a large log. After it was in place against the front cabin door, the captains voice came over the loudspeaker system telling us the temperature was seventy-five degrees and thanked everyone for flying the Sunshine Airline. I unfastened my seat belt, picked up my purse and small carryon bag, said goodbye to Mr. Bowen and followed the other passengers thru the tunnel and into the airport terminal.

After securing my luggage I hailed a cab and gave the driver the address. Yes—he said he knew of the Sunshine Sea Air Motel, a very nice place by the ocean. The driver wove in and out of traffic down to a road called "AIA". It was lined on either side by high condominiums. Past a park on our left, then another park on our right. Over a bridge that straddled a waterway from the ocean to the intercostals water. We proceeded past more high-rise buildings, some famous restaurants and motels that I had read about, a shopping center, then we came to a town. The cab driver said this was called Ocean Waves, as he passed store after store, I made mental notes of all the stores I would frequent once I was settled. He turned the corner and at the next traffic light made a left. A short distance later, he pulled the cab over to the curb and stopped. Here we were at the Sunshine Sea Air Motel. The driver placed my luggage on the porch step, I paid him while thanking him for all his information and said goodbye.

Pausing for a moment before going to the motel office, I looked around. It was a very attractive motel, with a well-kept garden, and a front porch complete with rocking chairs and chaises. There was a large pool in the back area. Just then a man came out of the office and introduced himself as David, the motel manager. David helped me with the luggage and checked my apartment to be sure there were enough towels and soap. I walked thru the rooms—the apartment consisted of a kitchen, living room and bedroom and bath carpeted floors, nice drapes on the windows and a wall to wall closet in the bedroom. The kitchen cabinets held a pretty set of dishes and a complete set of pots and pans, the drawers were lined with clean paper and there were utensils and a set of silverware. I was completely satisfied. I walked back to the office with David and handed him a check for the entire season of three months. He wrote a receipt and said any time I needed something please call him of his wife Shirley. I returned to my apartment and took off my shoes and the heavy clothes, put on a lounging robe and stretched out on the bed.

I must have dozed off. The doorbell was ringing. I glanced at the clock; it was four p.m. Oh My! I must have been tired. I got up went to the door—much to my surprise it was Brent Bowen. He wanted to take me out for dinner. I paused—thought about it then accepted his invitation. He had rented a car, at the airport for his stay in Florida. He had been in Florida before many times and knew of some good places to eat. He was staying at a motel only a block away. We had dinner then Brent took me for a scenic ride of the "AIA" from Miami up to Fort Lauderdale beach area. We stopped for a few cocktails at Pier 66 then he took me back to my motel. I thanked him and said goodnight.

For the next few weeks Brent took me on sight seeing tours. Every time I glanced at a brochure, he would pick it up and make reservations for two. The streets, stores, and houses were being decorated for Christmas. I bought some cards for my family and friends back home, wrote a little note on each on and mailed them in the local post office. I was beginning to feel a little bit blue, being away at holiday time. One day the office manager handed me a bunch of envelopes tied together, they were cards from home that Sally had forwarded down to my Florida address plus some letters. It sure felt good to get mail from home. I hung up the cards on the living room wall with scotch tape. Brent took me out for Christmas dinner and we celebrated New Year's Eve at one of the local nightspots. The floorshow was fantastic. The costumes were very colorful and the dancers were very artistic. New Year's Day I enjoyed sitting, by the pool and getting a sun tan.

For the next couple of weeks, I enjoyed the company of some women that also had come to Florida for the winter and were staying at the Sunshine Sea Air Motel. We exchanged stories of our families and pictures. There was Judy, a divorcee with three grown children. Florence, she had been a widow for ten years, and Marge, she had remained single. They all were from New Jersey what a small world! They all had some romantic encounters in the past few years but had backed away at the thought of marriage. I supposed they were right in the feeling the way they did. After all, between divorce, illness and whatever else, one does get "gunshy".

We all agreed on one subject strongly—we liked being independent, able to come and go as we pleased. Maybe that was a selfish feeling, but it was ours. The four of us became friends, we all were retired, with plenty of time on our hands. Of course, all of us had our minor ills, but for the most part, healthy enough to enjoy the relaxed place of retirement and indulge in some exciting travel. We went out to lunches, fashion shows, did some window shopping and of course purchased souvenirs.

I hadn't heard from Brent in almost a month. He did not seem the type to make a friendship then just walk away. I called his hotel phone and the manager said Mr. Bowen had left on a business trip but would return soon. I decided to do some extensive traveling this year. The motel manager had told me where the nearest travel bureau was. That morning while sunbathing by the pool I mentioned travelling to the three women. They were very interested, so, the four of us made a trip that afternoon into the town of Ocean Waves. We approached the travel agent with our ideas. She suggested a three-day cruise to start off with. After our arrangements were made for the last three days in January the agent gave us some brochures on longer cruises, some special flights the airlines were making to parts of Europe and the Orient. We thanked her and left. By now it was dinnertime so we stopped at the local restaurant. Judy ordered corned beef and cabbage and I had one of my favorites—borsch with sour cream and a hot pastramie plate. After dinner we walked back to the motel, for a little exercise.

That night I lay in bed thinking how lucky I was to have found friends this far from home. With that thought I drifted off into a deep sleep. When I awoke and looked out the window the sun was already high in the sky. My goodness! The clock on my night table read eleven a.m. As I put on my robe and slippers there was a knock on the door. I could see the shadow of a man thru the glazed glass. I quickly brushed my hair, splashed water on my face and then went to the door. There stood Brent with a bouquet of flowers. With many apologies he explained the sudden leave and reason why he had to travel unexpectedly. He asked me to join him for lunch and I agreed. I accepted his apologies and excused myself to get dressed while he waited on the porch. I showered and dressed in a blouse and slack outfit I had purchased in town, did my makeup, picked up my purse and apartment key and walked outside to join Brent. During the ride, he was unusually quiet. I tried making conversation and joking, this made me feel quite uneasy. Brent must have sensed this because he took my hand in his and squeezed gently and smiled. Now I felt a little better. He slowed the car and pulled into a parking lot next to the restaurant. As we walked thru the lot and around to the front entrance, I couldn't help notice how quaintly familiar it was. Why, it resembled the sidewalk café back home. Complete with the candy-striped umbrellas in the center of round tables and a little picket fence around the patio. It was almost noon, most of the tables were already taken. A cheerful waiter approached, spoke to Brent, then led us to a small table for two in the far corner. We ordered a cold mug of root beer with our lunch then began exchanging stories of the past month while waiting for our waiter to return. Brent had been on a necessary but interesting business trip, I explained about my three-day cruise I was going on with my new friends. We finished lunch, Brent tipped the waiter and we left. On the way home we stopped by a sweet-shoppe. The ice cream menu was so full of delicious rich gooie concoctions it was hard to choose one and not the other. I ordered a cherry vanilla sundae topped with cherries, nuts and whipped cream. Brent ordered a banana split that had three scoops of ice cream, nuts and whipped cream with chocolate topping. By the time we got back to the motel it was four thirty p.m. I thanked Brent for a lovely day. I reminded him of my cruise and that I wouldn't be back until February first. He promised to call me the night I returned from the cruise and told me to have a good time.

The following day Judy, Florence and Marge and I packed one suit case each plus a small bag. We had dinner together in our favorite town restaurant. We were so excited about going on the cruise we almost forgot to buy film for our cameras. We walked home after enjoying our favorite meals, stopping by the camera shop to purchase film. We relaxed on the lounge chairs on the porch of the motel and before retiring for the night we informed the manager of our three-day trip. He was very happy for us, wished us a safe return and assured us our apartments would be secure while we were gone. We all went to bed early, because we had to get up at five a.m. the cab would pick us up at six a.m. and the cruise line was to leave at seven a.m.

The next morning came too fast. I wasn't used to getting up this early. I fumbled in the dark for the bedroom light. After taking a nice warm shower, I dressed and had a cup of coffee. My luggage was by the door and I was anxious to get started. The manager rang our doorbells to be sure we were up and then helped with the luggage. The cab driver was right on time. It was a beautiful sunny day, with just a soft breeze blowing. I went back to my apartment for alight jacket and that roll of film I almost forgot. The ride to the cruise terminal seemed to take forever. It was a weekday morning and there was plenty of traffic. It was amazing, how the cab driver could weave in and out, past the congested areas, and stalled vehicles. Finally, we arrived at the Port of Miami. A short ride over the bridge and we were there. The driver pulled up to the curb of the terminal and placed our luggage at the terminal entrance. Judy took care of paying the driver while I hailed a baggage handler. He directed us upstairs and to the correct ticket booth. Once our reservations were stamped and returned to us, we proceeded to the ramp that led to our steamship.

By the time the four of us found our two staterooms, a porter had put out our luggage by the doors. We were fortunate to have outside cabins. Judy and I took a cabin and Florence and Marge took the other one. Our cabins were next to one another which was another lucky break. The porter explained he was stationed in our area and he was the one to call if we needed anything. The cabins had twin beds, a couch, night table and a long dresser with plenty of drawers. Clothes closet and a comfortably sized bathroom. On the night table was a bowl of fresh fruit and an itinerary of the three-day cruise. Just as we were starting to unpack there was a knock on the door. I answered, opening the door. Our porter was holding a silver bowl of ice containing a chilled bottle of champagne. I thank the porter and placed the silver bowl on the table. Attached to the bottle was a note—it was a bon voyage present from Brent. How sweet and thoughtful. Judy called Florence and Marge to come to our room. I opened the bottle and poured the bubbly champagne into four glasses. We toasted our cruise then toasted Brent. After we finished the champagne, we walked out on the deck to watch the cruise ship leave the port.

It was a very impressive sight. Our ship was huge, it appeared as a giant over the little private boats going and coming. We stood by the rail looking up and down the Miami beach, watching the tall buildings grow smaller as we sailed further out to sea. The breakfast bell rang and a voice came over the loudspeaker system requesting everyone that signed for early first seating to please proceed to the dining rooms. It was continental style, a breakfast of juice, danish, buns and coffee. When we were finished eating, the four of us returned to our cabins to unpack our bags. We then went back on deck. After walking the length of the ship, we decided to reserve four deck chairs on the stern deck out of the wind. A porter walking around the deck assured us the four chairs we had picked would be ours for the entire cruise. We thanked him and settled back to enjoy the sun and soft breeze coming across the stern of the ship. The ships bells rang and again an announcement was made, this time for lunch. We decided to forget about dieting while on our cruise. It would be near impossible to pass by all those delicious tempting platters of food and desserts. We had a table by one of the windows where we could see the waves and the seagulls flying by as we ate. After lunch we went looking for the beauty parlor and gift shop. We made appointments to have our hair washed and set, then we browsed around the gift shop purchasing a few souvenirs. Then back to the stern and our lounge chairs. We must have dozed off for a couple of hours. The cool chill air woke us up. The four of us had a combination sunburn and windburn. By the time we had showered and applied cream to our pink skin the dinner bell was sounding. We put on our very comfortable loose-fitting printed moo-moo's that we had purchased in some of the ships stores and joined the others for dinner. There were numerous appetizers, roast beef, ham, chicken, assorted freshly cooked vegetables, three different breads, gravies and then that tempting table of pastries. Oh My! I never in all my wildest dreams imagined the cruise meals would be this good. After dinner we walked around the deck for a while then went into one of the lounges for a few cocktails and to see the floor show. We must have gotten to bed about two a.m.

The next two days were full of fun. There was swimming in a large pool on one of the decks. Shuffleboard courts, skeet shooting, exercise classes, sauna rooms, a gambling casino, two lounges complete with entertainment and dance music every night, and those cute little stores where you could buy souvenirs ranging from post card, funny items, stuffed animals to beautiful imported crystal in shapes of animals, angels, birds and the exquisite and delicately painted vases. We had really taken advantage of as much as we could on our first cruise. After lunch on the final day we packed our bags, carefully packing the souvenirs so they wouldn't get broken. We placed the bags outside our doors filled out the envelopes on the night table and went out on deck for a while to relax on the lounge chairs. About four p.m. the ship eased into port and was secured by the work men on the dock. We disembarked—went thru a customs procedure and hailed a cab. The ride home was uneventful, not much traffic. The cab driver placed our luggage on the motel steps, we paid him and he drove off. It was almost six p.m. The four of us agreed we were tired and would just rest that evening and then see each other the next day. I carried my suitcase and bag to my apartment, unlocked the door, turned the lights and air conditioner on and then put the lock back door. After getting comfortable and having a cup of tea, I lay back on the couch to relax.

The phone rang—it was Brent—true to his word—he was calling as he had promised. I gave him a brief summary of my cruise. Yes, I really had a wonderful time and yes, I would go on a longer cruise if the opportunity arose. Brent wanted to take me out for dinner Friday night and to see a show. I begged off and asked for a rain check. I did not want to go anywhere for a week. I just want to catch my breath and relax. It had been such a wonderful three days, so full and so exhausting in a nice way. I was feeling unusually tired. Brent said he understood and I promised I would go out with him the following Friday, the second week of February. With that settled we both said goodnight.

The next week seemed to go as slow as a snails-pace. I was having a good time with my new friends, we enjoyed the motel pool, I wrote letters home to the family, we went to a fashion show, the beauty parlor for a new hair style and permanent. But something was missing. Deep inside me there inside me there was a lonely empty feeling. A feeling new to me. I had to admit to myself I really missed Brent, even for a week. This was not like me—I had never held a relationship with a man friend long enough to get close and involved. I had always wanted to have a good time, have friends, but stay independent. I had seen some very sweet marriages turn sour and I vowed this would never happen to me.

Friday was here, I rested by the pool all afternoon. Judy, Florence, and Marge had taken a day cruise on the intercostals waterway and wouldn't return until nighttime. About four p.m. I showered and dressed. Brent was right on time at five p.m. We had a lovely dinner and enjoyed a wonderful show. On the way back to the motel, Brent said he wanted to ask me something. Would I care for a cup of coffee? Yes, I would. We stopped at the little sidewalk café. While waiting for our coffee to be served, Brent reach into his pocket and pulled out a little blue velvet box and handed it to me. I opened the box and there was a diamond ring sparkling back at me. It was the largest rectangle shaped diamond I had ever seen. The stone was set high on a white gold filigree mounting. I was breathless—I didn't know what to say. I glanced up and my eyes met Brent's. They seemed to be begging for an answer. Fumbling for words he said he wanted me to be his girl—we wouldn't have to rush into marriage—just knowing that I felt about him the way he felt about me would be enough. I accepted the ring. Brent slipped it on my finger—it was a perfect fit. He reached across the table and gave me a kiss. At that moment the waiter appeared carrying our coffee. I'm sure I blushed as I sat back in my chair. We must have had a small audience for that scene. Everyone was clapping and some people even came over to our table wishing us happiness. Oh My! I was feeling like a young schoolgirl. Brent drove me back to the motel, giving me a gentle kiss before I got out of the car. He would call me tomorrow noon.

That night I could hardly sleep I was so excited. The next morning, I just had to call my family. I dialed Sally's number—no answer so I dialed Mary's number. The phone rang about six times. I was just about to hang up when Mary answered. She had just come in from shoveling snow, the New Jersey coast had its first big snow storm of the year. She was delighted about Brent and my engagement ring. Sally would call the others and tell them of my good news. I made sure she didn't build the news up to a coming marriage. Sally gave me all the up-to-date news about the family, then the children spoke to me for a few minutes. They had been building a snowman in the front yard. After sending my love to everyone, I promised to keep Sally informed of what was going on. After applying sun tan lotion generously, I slipped into my bathing suit and went out by the pool. My friends were already sunbathing. I decided to say "good morning", settle back on a lounge chair and wait until someone noticed my ring. I turned my hand purposely so the sunshine would sparkle off the diamond. It worked. As if by magic my friends all noticed the ring at the same time. After that, the questions came fast. They were very happy for me, of course they did a lot of kidding. No—I couldn't go out to lunch with them because I was expecting a call from Brent. The warm sun felt good, we had managed to find a spot by the pool where we would be out of the strong breeze, blocked by one half of the motel. That strong breeze blowing in from the East since we arrived in Florida. It certainly was better than staying up north for the snow and ice storms and slippery roads and sidewalks iced up with frozen snow. I had endured enough of that and now that I was retired, I vowed never to be up north again in the winter. My friends had the same idea also. Judy, Florence and Marge excused themselves. They were going out to lunch and then to a fashion show. I went back to my apartment to wait for the phone call.

Brent's call was right on time. He had been to a travel agent friend of his in the morning. There was a special trip going to Europe. He wanted to take me along. We would see Austria, France, Germany and Italy—we would be gone thirty-two days. He would give me time to think about it—all the rest of the afternoon. Brent would pick me up at four p.m. to take me to travel agent to make definite plans. I hung up the phone breathless with excitement and surprise. This was all coming too fast for me. I made myself a cup of tea and sat back and gave this proposed trip to some deep consideration. I had never ever thought about going abroad, especially for such a long time. That would be an awfully long time to be out of the United States. Brent was a truly wonderful person, and I was very fond of him, but to be that far away form my family gave me a little chill. Maybe I was being foolish, but after all I was no young girl either. If Brent would speak with my family and they agreed I would go. Yes, that was the right thing to do. When Brent came over at four p.m. I would explain to him how I felt and I would call the family. With that decision made I waited for Brent. I must have dozed off. The ringing of the doorbell woke me. It was Brent—precisely at four p.m. He was anxious for my answer. I told him of my feelings and he agreed. He was sorry if he had rushed me and yes, I was right to be concerned. We called up north and spoke to Sally. She thought it would be a wonderful trip. Then we called my nephew Larry. Brent spoke with him a long-time giving Larry and up-to-date account of what was happening. Then I spoke to Larry, he was very happy for us, he approved after giving Brent the "third degree". I promised to keep Larry posted on our departure date and what airlines and where we would be staying and when we would return. Larry said he would call Mary and Sue. With that settled we said good-bye and hung up the phone. I was so excited I could barely put the coffee pot on. Brent reminded me that we had to get back to the travel agent before the office closed. The agent was waiting for us when we walked into his office. After introductions, he explained we needed passports, medical checkup and some precautionary shots. Our trip was to start a week from Monday. He would help push thru the passports as a favor to Brent, we could use his family doctor for our physicals. Brent wrote the agent a check to cover both fares, included were side tours, hotel accommodations and two meals daily plus baggage handling and transportation to and from the airport. We left the agency excited but satisfied. We had a folder full of brochures, hints on what clothing to take and so on. We stopped in one of the favorite cafeterias on our way back and had a delightful meal, complete with cheesecake and coffee. Brent had some business to take care of again and I had a busy week ahead of me so we decided to make a date for next Saturday evening.

For the next couple of days, I sorted out my wardrobe, spent a few hours with my friends (they helped me make a list of items I needed to shop for). They were almost excited as much as I was. I decided to shop alone. I was so used to being independent that their help began to get a little annoying. It wasn't their fault—they were very sweet and meant well. I walked down to the shopping center and after a short while I decided to take a bus to one of the new shopping malls. I had found a few items but comparison-shopping was one of my habits. By Friday my shopping was done and by Saturday afternoon I was packed and ready for that European vacation. Brent and I enjoyed a dinner and show then stopped at our favorite café again for coffee. The waiter remembered us and brought a complimentary pot of coffee to our table. I was home by midnight. The next day I just stayed indoors and rested. It had been a whirlwind of a week and I needed to catch my breath. There was plenty to eat in my refrigerator although I wasn't feeling very hungry. There were some good stories on television and that evening I managed to write some letters to my family.

Monday morning, I was up early and ready to leave. Brent came over for a cup of coffee while we waited for the cab. For the next thirty days, we toured the cities and countryside of Austria, France, Germany and Italy. We met interesting people, we ate food indigenous to the particular geographic areas, took pictures and all in all had a marvelous time. I was tired but happy.

Brent was beginning to look quite worn out. The morning we were due to pack for our return home I called his room. There was no answer. I walked down the hall and knocked on his door, it was partially open. I looked in and there was Brent lying on the floor by his packed suitcases. The hotel manager called a doctor but it was too late. Brent had suffered a fatal heart attack. The doctor explained that the trip was too much for his weak heart. On the night table were four bottles of medicines. Brent had never said anything about his heart problem.

I was in shock until our group returned home. His agent friend was notified and he took care of all the arrangements. Then I was called to attend a special meeting at a lawyer's office. It concerned Brent's will. Now why should I be called to that meeting? To my astonishment, Brent had made a new will while in Florida and had made provisions for me financially. After the technical part of the will being read, I had to sign some papers. I was to receive a lump sum of all Brent's assets. He had no living relations and had stated in the will that I was the only person close to him. The lawyer assured me that he would handle the details and that a letter from his office with a check would be sent up north to my home. Sadness had enveloped me.

My friends tried to console me and tried to plan outings to take my mind off my grief but to no avail.

I called my family and told them what happened and that I was coming home. Larry said he would meet me at the airport, and to let him know as soon as I had made my reservations on the airline.

This winter vacation surely had been full of TRAVEL JOY and SORROW.

9

RETURNING HOME

The March winds were blowing when I arrived back in New Jersey. Larry explained he had to go on a sales trip but Debbie and the children would stay with me for a while. For the first time in years, I didn't want to be alone. Debbie was so sweet and thoughtful. She did the cooking and cleaning and for the next two weeks I just sat around, feeling sorry for myself, and missing Brent's smile and quick humor. One day some of my friends that had since retired stopped by for a visit. They had sold their homes and moved into condominiums. Would I please visit with them next week? I thanked them and accepted their invitation. By now Debbie had returned to her home. I convinced her that I was fine now and no need for her to worry. From there on I was busy with visiting and having friends in for lunch.

The new life style at the condominiums was very tempting. After all, there was no more gardening to do. No outside painting and fixing up, no lawn to keep mowed. There was a large heated pool, sauna, exercise classes, hobby classes, weekly dances and social lunches, bingo and card games. There was one day I almost weakened. There was a two-bedroom condo with three views. It was a fourth-floor corner apartment. The kitchen was smartly decorated in white and black trim. Next to the oven and microwave combination was a cut out pass thru for serving dishes to

59

the dining room area. The living room was part of the dining area and led to a second-in balcony used as a porch and very attractively decorated. The two bedrooms and both bathrooms were off the hallway. There were Bahama fans in each room. There was a central air conditioning and heating system. Off the hallway was a huge walk in closet. The linen closet and storage area were on the opposite wall. The condo apartment had just come available. The owner was moving to Arizona, she was a widow and wanted to be near family.

After debating with myself for a few days I decided against the move. I had a lovely home that had been passed down to me from my parents. The home was a large and comfortable and held many fond memories. I talked it over with my family. They all wanted me to keep the homestead. The men had gotten together, surveyed the house in and out and made a list of repairs and replacements needed. They insisted it would again be their pleasure to help and they wouldn't think of letting me pay for the materials.

For the next six months there was lumber, tools and paint buckets everywhere. Every weekend the men worked on the house while my nieces and I tried to keep the children out of the way. We took them shopping, spent time in our local park and went to movies. Meals were prepared at Debbie's. By the end of September, all the work was completed, tools were picked up and excess materials and just plain junk was cleaned up and carted away.

The house looked beautiful. It was brand spanking new—inside and out. The roof had been replaced, new plumbing was installed, a new baseboard electric heating system installed. The walls were newly painted, and the outside had a new coat of paint also. The old screened porch had new combination aluminum windows with screens and new doors. A contractor friend of my nephew installed a central air conditioning unit.

With many hugs, kisses and tears of happiness I thanked my family for all they had done for me. Yes! I truly was glad I had kept this old wonderful homestead. There would be many more happy years to come, because I was RETURNING HOME.

My daydreaming on that Monday morning long ago had been A LIFE REMEMBERED.

THE END